# PLANT BASED DIET

..............................

## The 101 Best Whole Foods To Prevent Disease and Live Longer

## Health Research Staff

Published by:

Millwood Media
PO Box 1220
Melrose, FL 32666 USA

ISBN13: 978-1-937918-77-4

## Health Disclaimer

Any and all information contained herein is not intended to take the place of medical advice from a health care professional. Any action taken based on these contents is at the sole discretion and sole liability of the reader.

Readers should always consult appropriate health professionals on any matter relating to their health and well being before taking any action of any kind concerning health related issues. Any information or opinions provided here or in any Millwood Media related articles, materials or information are believed to be accurate and sound, however Millwood Media assumes no liability for the use or misuse of information provided by Millwood Media.

No personnel or associates of Millwood Media will in any way be held responsible by any reader who fails to consult the appropriate health authorities with respect to their individual health care before acting on or using any information contained herein, and neither the author or publisher of any of this information will be held responsible for errors or omissions, or use or misuse of the information.

# Table of Contents

Introduction......................v

1. Acai Berries ...................... 1
2. Apples ........................... 1
3. Apricots ......................... 3
4. Asparagus ........................ 3
5. Arugula .......................... 5
6. Artichoke ........................ 5
7. Avocados ......................... 5
8. Banana ........................... 6
9. Bamboo shoots .............. 6
10. Basil ........................... 7
11. Beets............................ 7
12. Bell peppers................... 8
13. Blackberries.................... 8
14. Blackcurrant ................ 10
15. Bean sprouts ............... 10
16. Beet root ..................... 11
17. Bok Choy...................... 11
18. Boysenberries ............. 13
19. Blueberries ................. 13
20. Broccoli ...................... 14
21. Broccolini .................. 14
22. Brussels sprouts .......... 15
23. Butter Leaf lettuce ...... 15
24. Cabbage ...................... 16
25. Cantaloupe .................. 16
26. Carrots ....................... 17

27. Cauliflower ................. 18
28. Celery ......................... 18
29. Cherry ......................... 19
30. Chicory ....................... 19
31. Chili pepper ............... 20
32. Chinese broccoli ........ 20
33. Chinese cabbage ........ 21
34. Chives ......................... 21
35. Collard greens ........... 22
36. Corn ............................ 22
37. Crab-apple .................. 24
38. Cranberry ................... 24
39. Cucumber ................... 25
40. Current ....................... 25
41. Dill.............................. 27
42. Eggplant ..................... 27
43. Fennel ......................... 28
44. Figs ............................. 28
45. Grapefruit ................... 29
46. Grapes ........................ 29
47. Gooseberry ................. 31
48. Green beans................. 31
49. Green peas .................. 32
50. Green pepper ............. 32
51. Honeydew ................... 33
52. Iceberg lettuce ........... 33
53. Kale............................. 34

54. Kiwi .................................. 34

55. Leeks ............................. 36

56. Lemon ........................... 36

57. Limes ............................ 37

58. Lychee ........................... 37

59. Mandarins ................... 39

60. Mushrooms ................. 39

61. Mustard Greens .......... 40

62. Oak leaf lettuce .......... 40

63. Olives ............................ 41

64. Onions ......................... 42

65. Oranges ....................... 43

66. Papaya .......................... 44

67. Paprika ........................ 44

68. Parsnip ......................... 45

69. Parsley........................... 45

70. Passion fruit ................ 46

71. Pears.............................. 47

72. Peppermint.................. 47

73. Pineapple ..................... 49

74. Plums ........................... 49

75. Pomegranate .............. 50

76. Prunes........................... 50

77. Pumpkin ..................... 51

78. Potatoes ....................... 52

79. Radish .......................... 52

80. Radicchio ..................... 55

81. Raisins .......................... 55

82. Raspberries ................. 55

83. Red pepper ................. 56

84. Romaine lettuce .......... 56

85. Rosemary ..................... 57

86. Sage .............................. 57

87. Seaweed ....................... 58

88. Snow peas .................... 58

89. Spaghetti squash ......... 61

90. Spinach ........................ 61

91. Strawberries ................. 62

92. Summer squash .......... 62

93. Swiss chard ................. 65

94. Tomatoes ..................... 65

95. Turnips ........................ 66

96. Turnip greens .............. 66

97. Watermelon ................. 67

98. Wasabi .......................... 68

99. Watercress ................... 68

100. Winter squash .......... 69

101. Yams ........................... 69

**Where to Find the 101
Best Whole Foods In Your
Grocery Store................ 71**

**Plant-Based Eating Can
Reap Rewards ................ 75**

**Tips For Eating Healthy
When Eating Out........... 81**

**References ...................... 85**

# Introduction

If you're someone who's looking to take control over your health, improve your energy levels, decrease your risk of disease, and make sure you aren't putting anything in your body that could cause you harm, you'll want to start making the switch over to plant-based foods.

One of the biggest problems in the diets of most people today is the fact that so much of our food consumption comes from processed meats and packaged foods. Not only will this cause the body's natural pH balance to shift, setting you up for problems, but it's also going to cause you to place a high number of toxins in your body that will end up damaging your organs, causing blood sugar instability, and could even impact the way your brain functions. By making the shift over to foods that are entirely natural, you eliminate the probability of these problems from ever occurring.

If you've seen the outstanding documentary *Forks Over Knives* you know its premise that "most, if not all, of the degenerative diseases that afflict us can be controlled, or even reversed, by rejecting our present menu of animal-based and processed foods." (If you haven't seen the film and you're contemplating a plant-based diet, it's a must-watch. Rent it tonight). The film gives an important overview of the 20-year China-Cornell-Oxford Project that led to findings that a number of diseases can be linked to the Western diet of processed and animal-based foods.

In addition to improving your health, eating in this manner will help you control your body weight as you'll naturally start to take in fewer and fewer calories each day.

Let's have a look at 101 of the best foods to be eating as part of your plant-based diet plan.

\* \* \* \* \*

**Attention All Eagle Eyes:** We've had a number of people proof this book before we released it to you, but there is a chance you might spot something that was missed. If you find a typo or other obvious error please send it to us. And if you're the first one to report it, we'll send you a free gift! Send to: millwoodmedia@gmail.com.

\* \* \* \* \*

# The 101 Best Whole Foods To Prevent Disease and Live Longer

# Acai Berries

One food that has quickly caught on as being one of the healthiest that you can consume is the Acai berry. You'll most traditionally find acai berries incorporated into juices or supplements, so turn to these items to reap the health benefits they provide. Acai berry is high in antioxidants and can help reduce inflammation and boost the immune system, as found in a study published in the Journal of Agriculture Food Chemistry. They contain essential fatty acids, and will also help improve insulin sensitivity.

# Apples

Apples are a great food for calming your hunger pains when they strike as they contain almost 15% of your total daily dietary fiber needs per apple. In addition to this, they also can help encourage a healthier digestive tract due to the type of bacteria that they contain. Just be sure that you eat the apples with the skin on as this is where many of the nutrients they contain are found.

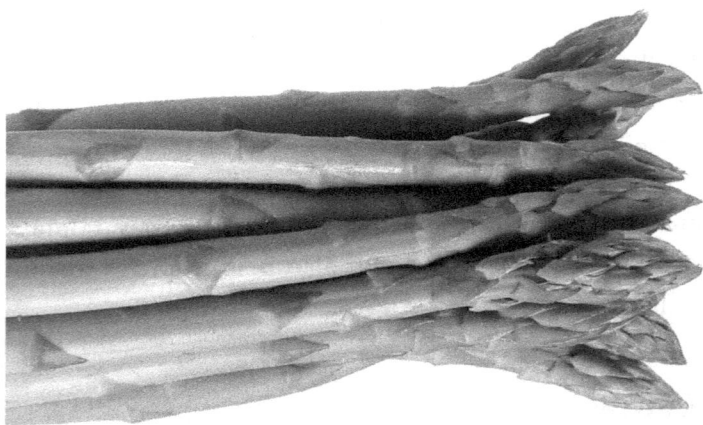

# Apricots

The apricot makes for a sweet treat any time you want something to snack on, and at only 16 calories per apricot, won't ruin anyone's diet plan. This fruit is rich in vitamin A and C content, and will also provide some potassium to help regulate muscle contractions and tryptophan for healthy muscle growth. Try topping your next bowl of cereal with some apricots for a burst of flavor.

# Asparagus

Asparagus is a very low calorie vegetable to include in your diet with one cup providing just 26 calories total towards your daily calorie requirement. Asparagus is a rich source of vitamin K, which is essential for ensuring your blood clots properly, and is also high in vitamin A, folate, iron, as well as vitamin B1. In addition to that, asparagus is a natural diuretic so if you happen to be retaining extra water, it may help you shed that water in a hurry.

# Arugula

Arugula is a form of lettuce that is often overlooked by many people but that provides strong nutritional benefits. This lettuce is low in calories, cholesterol free, and will provide you with thiamin, riboflavin, vitamin B6, zinc, and copper. It's also a good source of dietary fiber, so will help keep your hunger under control for longer periods of time.

# Artichoke

If you're looking for a new vegetable to try out, consider the artichoke. This vegetable is low in calories at just 60 per artichoke, and is also low in sodium as well. It's a great source of fiber, magnesium, and folate, and will also supply some vitamin C to help promote a stronger immune system. It works great as a side dish so make sure you don't forget to include it in your diet plan.

# Avocados

To help boost your healthy fat for the day, consider turning to avocados. These are rich in powerful unsaturated fatty acids that will keep your brain and organs working optimally. This food is also a great source of vitamin K, folate, vitamin C, vitamin B5, potassium, as well as vitamin B6, and will help defend against free radical damage in your body.

# Banana

If you want an energy packed snack on the go, turn to a banana. Bananas are high in potassium and starch, which means they are great for fueling intense workout sessions and can help keep blood pressure levels lower, as found by a study published in the Hypertension Journal. This food also tends to be very easy on the stomach, so it's a great option if you're experiencing mild upset stomach. With the high potassium content this food provides, it's an excellent way to protect against cardiovascular disease.

# Bamboo shoots

One food that most people never even consider adding to their diet that you may want to give some thought to is the bamboo shoot. Bamboo shoots are incredibly low in cholesterol, a great source of dietary fiber, and are also rich in riboflavin, zinc, as well as potassium, copper, and manganese. This food works great in stir fries, but is higher in sodium so be sure to watch your serving size.

# Basil

One of the best ways to add flavor to your foods without adding any additional calories is with basil. Basil is a good source of vitamin E, riboflavin, niacin, and is also an excellent way to increase your dietary fiber intake, while boosting your consumption of vitamin K, vitamin B6, folate, calcium, and iron. For such a simple herb, it will really pack a nutritional punch.

# Beets

Beets are one food that contain a high amount of phytonutrients, making them excellent for warding off free radical damage from exposure to daily toxins. Eating beets on a regular basis can help provide strong anti-inflammatory support, and help ward off diseases such as diabetes. In addition to this, they can also help detoxify your body, cleansing your system and helping you feel better on a day-to-day basis.

# Bell peppers

Bell peppers are a fantastic way to boost your immune system due to their very high vitamin C content. Additionally, they are a flavorful way to add more variety to your dishes, and will also supply a small dose of dietary fiber. Adding these to your diet can also help prevent the development of cancer due to the antioxidants that they contain. Finally, one study noted that a diet containing bell peppers might promote an increase in the rate of learning, so they may have positive benefits on cognitive capabilities as well.

# Blackberries

If you want a food that's high in fiber to help calm your appetite, turn to blackberries. Blackberries are not only rich in fiber content, but are also a great source of vitamin C, vitamin K, and manganese. This food will also provide you with some folate, helping ensure that you experience proper cell growth and cell division.

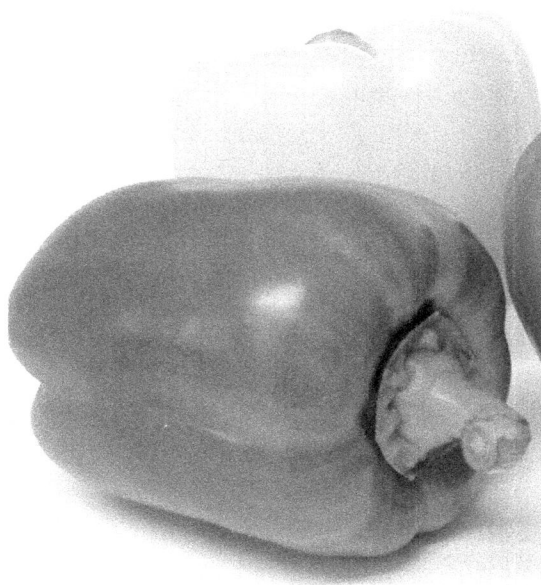

# Blackcurrant

Blackcurrants are a food that offers great health benefits as they can help ward against cancer, aging, and inflammation, while also helping to protect your immune system with a strong dose of vitamin C. Blackcurrants are also high in iron content, which will help ensure that you don't suffer from fatigue during exercise. Iron-deficiency anemia is a big health concern among many people and blackcurrants can help you overcome this problem.

# Bean sprouts

Bean sprouts are a great source of carbs in the diet and are relatively low in calories as well. Coming in at just 53 calories per cup, you can certainly fit these into your daily diet without a problem. Bean sprouts are rich in vitamin B6, pantothenic acid, iron, magnesium, as well as phosphorus, and are also a good way to get your folate in as well. With 119% of your daily requirement for vitamin C, you'll quickly meet your needs with this food.

# Beet root

Beet root is one food that will provide you with strong antioxidant protection, safeguarding you from free radical damage. In addition to that, it also helps to work as an anti-inflammatory for the body and can help provide strong detoxification support. It will promote healthy liver function and will also help reduce your risk of cardiovascular disease. Finally, one study also noted that beet root can act as a preventative strategy for cancer as well.

# Bok Choy

Bok Choy is a Chinese vegetable that is often added to Chinese dishes and sometimes into soups or stir-fries. Just like any other vegetable, bok choy provides powerful health benefits. Per 100 grams, this vegetable only contains 13 calories, so you don't even need to add it to your daily calorie intake after eating it. In addition to that, it's also a great source of anti-oxidants, vitamin C, vitamin K, as well as vitamin A, making it an all-around healthy addition to any diet plan. Finally, it'll also provide a small amount of calcium as well, which can go a long way towards helping you maintain stronger bones.

# Boysenberries

Boysenberries contain 66 calories per cup and will provide you with 7 grams of dietary fiber, making them one of the best high-fiber foods that you could consume. In addition to their fiber content, they're also rich in vitamin C, iron, calcium, and manganese, and will support high energy levels. Low in sodium, this is the perfect food for someone who wants to promote heart health.

# Blueberries

Blueberries are rich in vitamin K, manganese, as well as vitamin C, and are also a very good source of dietary fiber that will help tide your hunger over until your next meal. Blueberries contain a high number of antioxidants and will help protect against inflammation and free radical damage. In addition to that, blueberries are also one of the healthiest foods that you could eat to promote a healthy mind. Blueberries are great for boosting brainpower and reducing age-related mental decline, as found by a study in the Journal of Agricultural and Food Chemistry.

# Broccoli

One of the most nutritionally dense foods that you can add to your diet program is broccoli. Broccoli is great for lowering your cholesterol level, providing strong detoxification support, and will also help to reduce the level of oxidative stress you experience on a daily basis. In addition to that, broccoli can also improve the health of your digestive system and offer strong cardiovascular support.

# Broccolini

Broccolini is a smaller version of the usual broccoli that most people add into their diet programs. It's going to offer very similar nutritional content, being rich in vitamin A, C, as well as K, while giving off strong antioxidant support. The main difference between broccolini and broccoli comes in the taste as broccolini offers a slightly sweeter taste. In addition to that, it also cooks more rapidly than regular broccoli, so works great for those days when you need a meal on the go.

# Brussels sprouts

The one vegetable that many people claim to hate will actually provide you with a large number of health benefits that you should be very aware of. Brussels sprouts are great for helping lower your cholesterol level and will also help detox your system, reducing all the waste build-up that's accumulated over time. Brussels sprouts are going to provide strong anti-inflammatory benefits, which can reduce the risk of disease associated with inflammation, and will enhance your digestive system as well.

# Butter Leaf lettuce

Butter leaf lettuce is one variety of lettuce that you may want to consider if your salads need a little livening up. This variety of lettuce provides just 10 calories per cup and will offer almost one gram of dietary fiber per serving. It's also a good source of vitamin A, vitamin K, and will provide you with a small amount of calcium as well.

# $C$abbage

One vegetable that is often termed a nutritional 'powerhouse' because it is so nutrient dense is cabbage. Cabbage stands out for its cancer-fighting properties, especially warding off lung, stomach, colon, and rectal cancer as noted by a study published in the Cancer Epidemiology Journal. Cabbage will provide you with a serious dose of vitamin K, vitamin C, folate, as well as manganese and vitamin B6. In addition to that, it's also a terrific source of calcium, and vitamin B1. Cabbage can be added to salads, stir-fries, or made into soup as it's commonly used.

# $C$antaloupe

Cantaloupe is a sweet fruit that tastes great when at the perfect ripeness, and will provide well over 100% of both your vitamin A and vitamin C requirements. In addition to that, it will also supply you with a good dose of dietary fiber, niacin, vitamin B6, as well as folate, and will help contribute to your daily potassium requirement.

# Carrots

Carrots are one of the more commonly eaten vegetables in the diet and are loaded with good nutrition. They are slightly higher in calories and carbohydrates than many other vegetables, but are still quite low in calories overall coming in at 50 per cup. They are also a very rich source of vitamin A, vitamin K, vitamin C, potassium, B vitamins, and folate. Finally, carrots will help to promote healthy eye-sight, shielding you against night blindness.

# Cauliflower

One vegetable that you can be sure will support optimal health is cauliflower. This vegetable is part of the cruciferous vegetable family and will provide you with an excellent dose of vitamin C, vitamin K, folate, vitamin B6, as well as potassium. It's known to be excellent for helping to reduce your risk of developing cancer and will also help detoxify your system. This is a terrific food for anyone to eat that is worried about the development of Crohn's disease, inflammatory bowel disease, as well as insulin resistance.

# Celery

Celery is an incredibly low calorie vegetable containing just 16 calories per cup, with many of those calories coming from dietary fiber. It is actually considered to be "negative" in calories because your body burns more calories to break it down than the celery actually contains! It's also going to provide you with a great source of vitamin K, folate, vitamin A, as well as potassium, and will even provide a small amount of calcium to strengthen your bones. Celery is also great for anyone who wants to lower their blood pressure, so it's also good for those who are concerned with heart health.

# Cherry

Cherries are another one of the sweeter fruits that you may choose to eat, and are rated very low in the glycemic index scale, meaning they will have minimal impact on your blood glucose levels. Cherries are also a great source of dietary fiber and will help you meet your daily intake requirements for vitamin C. Cherries are great when eaten on their own, or try them stirred into a bowl of Greek yogurt for a sweet snack on the go.

# Chicory

Chicory is a type of lettuce that will add a unique flavor to any salad you serve up and is also going to provide you with a number of nutrients including thiamin, niacin, zinc, vitamin A, vitamin C, vitamin E, vitamin K, folate, calcium, iron, and magnesium. This lettuce variety is also a good source of potassium, which can help ensure a regular heart beat and proper blood pressure.

# Chili Pepper

Chili peppers are unique in that not only will they help increase the taste of many of the dishes that you're preparing, but in addition to that they will also increase your total daily calorie burn as well. Chili peppers will cause the body to expend more energy in the form of heat after you consume them, which in turn means that you have an easier time maintaining your body weight. Furthermore, those who eat spicy foods containing chili pepper often don't consume as much food during that meal, so this also means that they lower their overall calorie consumption.

# Chinese broccoli

Chinese broccoli is a broccoli variety that looks very much like lettuce and ranks low on the calorie count scale at just 19 per one cup serving. Chinese broccoli is rich in vitamin E, vitamin B6, iron, phosphorus, zinc, copper, and is also a fantastic source of dietary fiber, vitamin A, and vitamin C. it will even provide you with 9% of your total calcium intake. If you don't consume many dairy products in your everyday diet, this is one food that you may want to eat more regularly.

# $C$hinese cabbage

Chinese cabbage offers a unique taste experience from regular cabbage and can be sautéd, stir-fried, or baked with ease. This cabbage variety will provide just 9 calories per cup and is low in sodium with just 46 mg per serving. It will provide just over 50% of your daily total vitamin C requirement and 63% of your vitamin A needs. In addition to that, it also supplies you with some magnesium, potassium, and manganese, which all support a healthy heart and vital organ functioning.

# $C$hives

Chives are an excellent low calorie way to add more flavor to your food and help boost your nutritional intake as well. Chives support a healthy digestive system and also offer some strong anti-cancer fighting benefits as well. In addition to that, they'll also supply you with calcium, beta-carotene, vitamin K, as well as potassium. For a quick way to liven up any meal, make sure you give chives a try.

# $\mathcal{C}$ollard greens

Collard greens are a terrific food to help lower the total level of cholesterol in your body, while also helping to provide detoxification support. Collard greens are high in vitamin K, vitamin A, Vitamin C, folate, manganese, and will also provide you with some calcium as well. Best of all, this food is very low in calories at just 49 per cup, so it's an easy add to any diet plan.

# $\mathcal{C}$orn

Corn is a vegetable enjoyed by many as it offers a sweeter taste than most vegetables. Being that it is sweeter, it is slightly higher in total sugar content, but don't let that deter you. The high fiber content helps balance this out, so you won't experience too large of an insulin spike from eating it, as noted in a study published in 2007. Corn is also rich in vitamin C, vitamin B3, as well as manganese, and provides strong antioxidant benefits as well.

# Crab-apple

Crab apples offer a nice alternative for someone who wants to try something a little different with their diet plan, and go for a more tart taste than the regular apple possesses. Crab-apples, just like regular apples, are rich in vitamin C, high in dietary fiber, and are also low in sodium and cholesterol free. They do contain some sugar, but being natural fruit sugar, is much healthier for the body.

# Cranberry

One of the most notable benefits that the cranberry offers is strong protection against urinary tract infections. Cranberries have been often used as a treatment for anyone suffering from a UTI, and some people also choose to use them for preventative support as well. Cranberries are rich in vitamin C content, high in fiber, and will also supply you with a good dose of vitamin K and vitamin E as well. At just 23 calories per half cup, you definitely can't go wrong adding this to your plan.

# Cucumber

Cucumbers are a good food to add into your diet if you're watching your weight because they are so low in calories, yet high in water content, so they'll really help to encourage optimal fat loss success because you will feel more full when eating them. They will provide you with 21.3% of your total vitamin K needs and also supply you with plenty of molybdenum, vitamin C, and potassium as well. Being that they do contain so much water, they'll help with hydration also.

# Current

While some people traditionally prefer black currents, others would prefer to eat red or white currents instead. Currents are a rich source of dietary fiber, providing five grams per one cup serving and will also provide a small amount of protein as well. In addition to this, they're high in vitamin C content, will provide 6% of your daily iron needs, and will also provide you with manganese as well as potassium.

# Dill

Dill is another great way to add more flavor to your dishes and will also enhance your overall nutritional standing as well. Dill contains a good dose of calcium, manganese, iron, fiber, as well as magnesium; so many important minerals that the body needs to function optimally. Dill can also help to prevent the spread of bacteria in your body, which will reduce the risk of developing various illnesses as well. Finally, the combination of iron, manganese, and calcium will go a long way towards preventing bone loss.

# Eggplant

One standout property of eggplant that's worth noting is the fact that it will help to promote a healthy mind. Eggplant contains nasunin, which is an antioxidant that will help keep your brain membranes safe from free radical damage. In addition to that, eggplant is also high in antioxidants and can reduce the impact of antioxidant stress on the body. One study also noted eggplant is also great for providing strong cardiovascular health benefits so is ideal for those who are hoping to keep their heart healthy.

# Fennel

Fennel is a terrific vegetable to eat if you want to promote a stronger immune system due to its high vitamin C content. Vitamin C acts as a strong antioxidant in the body and will assist with the defending of any free radicals you happen to encounter. Fennel is also a fantastic source of fiber and folate, so can help to promote a strong cardiovascular system as well.

# Figs

Figs offer a very unique taste that most fruits and vegetables don't quite compare to. Figs help decrease your blood pressure, and improve circulation. They are very rich in potassium, which is an important mineral that is involved with blood pressure regulation, and are also extremely high in fiber. This dietary fiber will help to produce a feeling of satiety in the body, so if you're looking for weight control, figs are an excellent choice. Finally, if you eat the leaves, you can also help to reduce the amount of total insulin that your body is producing.

# Grapefruit

Grapefruits are often touted for their weight loss benefits and while they definitely will help you lose weight, it's not because of any magical property they possess. Instead, grapefruits are simply low in calories and high in nutrients, and make for a great addition to any diet plan. Grapefruits are rich in vitamin C, vitamin A, will also pack in a small dose of fiber, and as noted by numerous studies, can also help to protect against cancer. At 60 calories per grapefruit, they won't bump up your total daily calorie intake by all that much either.

# Grapes

Grapes are well known for their resveratrol content, which is a compound that helps to ward off cancer and promote a healthy heart. In addition to this, grapes also rank low on the GI scale, so they won't increase blood sugar levels as much as other foods, and will keep you satisfied between meals when you eat them. With the high number of antioxidants that grapes possess, you'll also be doing your part to defend against as much free radical damage as possible.

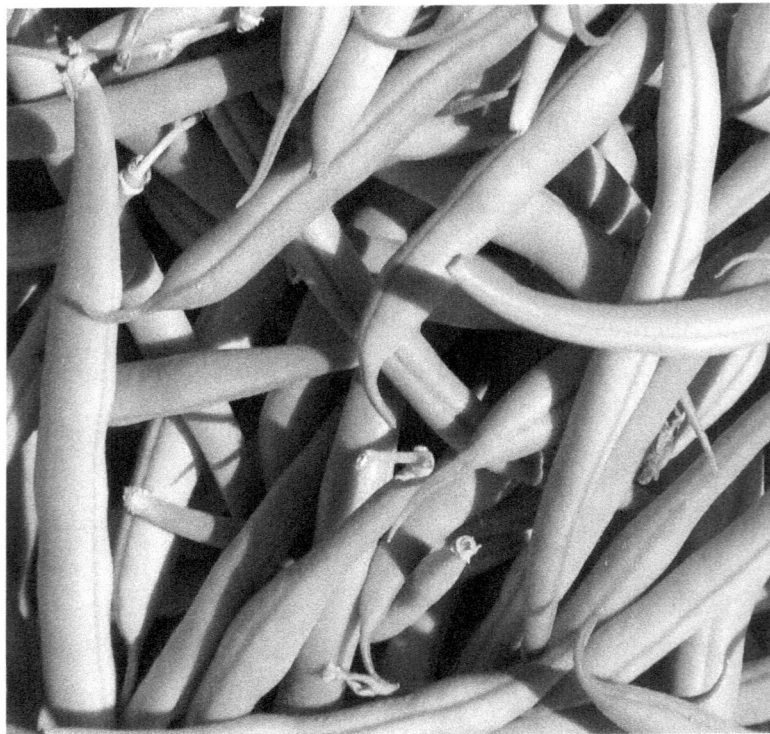

# Gooseberry

Gooseberries are a type of berry that is only rarely eaten by most individuals, but does pack a powerful health punch. This berry is high in vitamin A, potassium, manganese, as well as vitamin C, and will also provide 6 grams of fiber per cup. Gooseberries offer a nice unique taste and will be a great addition to any bowl of yogurt or cereal.

# Green beans

Green beans are a relatively low calorie food to include in your diet plan and will provide you with a great source of riboflavin, calcium, iron, magnesium, phosphorus, potassium, as well as vitamin A and vitamin K. In addition to that, you'll also take in five grams of dietary fiber per cup of green beans consumed, which will help to keep hunger levels under control and blood sugar levels regulated.

# Green peas

Green peas contain a type of phytonutrient that tends to be especially helpful in reducing your risk of Type 2 Diabetes and can also help to decrease the overall level of inflammation occurring in the body as well. Green peas are high in vitamin K, which is a key nutrient for improving blood clotting ability, and are also rich in manganese, vitamin C, fiber, and vitamin B1. Finally, you'll consume over 10% of both your zinc and iron content when consuming green peas.

# Green pepper

Green peppers are a great way to get in your vitamin C requirements, as one cup will provide 200% of your daily needs. In addition to that, green peppers are also high in vitamin A content, provide a small dose of iron, and will also help to boost your immune system. They quickly add flavor to any dish you're preparing.

# Honeydew

Honeydew is a fruit that is low in calories at just 64 per cup, but will provide a good dose of vitamin C, at 53% of your total daily requirements. In addition to that, honeydew is also rich in folate and potassium, which will help to promote healthy blood pressure levels. While there is a higher amount of natural fruit sugars in honeydew, because they are natural to the body, they will help to decrease hunger rather than increase it.

# Iceberg lettuce

Iceberg lettuce is one of the lowest calorie foods you can consume with just 10 calories per one cup serving. In addition to that, it's also high in Thiamin, vitamin B6, iron, as well as potassium, and is a great source of dietary fiber, vitamin A, as well as vitamin C. Iceberg lettuce is a fantastic foundation to a salad when combined with other leafy greens such as Romaine lettuce or spinach.

# Kale

Kale is another food that works great to help reduce your chances of developing UTI's and will also provide excellent detoxification support for your body as well. Kale is a fantastic source of vitamin K, vitamin A, as well as vitamin C, and will also provide you with a good dose of manganese as well. In addition to this, kale can help to boost your bone health due to its calcium content and will keep energy levels higher during exercise since it contains iron. Finally, one study published in the Carcinogenesis Journal noted that kale is particularly helpful at warding off the development of bladder cancer.

# Kiwi

Kiwi is a fruit that is going to provide you with some very strong antioxidant protection, and can provide support against diseases such as colon cancer, atherosclerosis, as well as heart disease. Kiwi is going to go a long way towards helping you control your blood sugar levels while also promoting optimal cardiovascular health and contains just 45 calories per small fruit. Finally, kiwi can help prevent macular degeneration; so if that's a condition you're concerned about then kiwi is an addition worth considering in your diet.

# Leeks

If you want serious cardiovascular support, consider turning to leeks to help you out. Leeks help boost the natural production of nitric oxide in the body as noted by a study published in the Journal of Pharmacology, which can help to relax the blood vessels leading to, and from the heart, which in turn improves blood circulation. In addition to this, leeks can also help to reduce the level of oxidative stress that you experience that can lead to chronic low-levels of inflammation. This can help you ward off health conditions such as Type 2 Diabetes, obesity, as well as rheumatoid arthritis.

# Lemon

Many people never stop to consider adding lemons to their diet, but this food can offer some significant health benefits worth knowing about. First, it's very low in calories at just 15 per quarter cup. In addition to that, lemons also help boost the level of antioxidant support that you're experiencing while defending against rheumatoid arthritis development. Just a hint of lemon will quickly add flavor to any dish that you're preparing.

# Limes

Limes are another great way to boost the flavor of any dish that you're creating, and improve your health in the process. Limes are also high in antioxidant content, which will protect against free radical damage. In addition to this, they also can help to promote healthier cholesterol levels in the body, and promote optimal heart health.

# Lychee

The lychee is an oriental fruit that contains 125 calories per cup and will also provide you with 2 grams of dietary fiber. This fruit is very high in vitamin C content, providing you 226% of your overall daily needs and will also provide some copper as well. As the fruit contains no cholesterol and is very low in sodium, it's great for those looking to promote heart health as well.

# Mandarins

Mandarins are a sweet treat that will provide a break from the regular orange, and are also high in dietary fiber and vitamin C content. Mandarin oranges will help to support a healthy immune system due to the vitamin C content they include and help prevent you from developing the common cold or flu.

# Mushrooms

Mushrooms are an excellent vegetable to eat that will help to boost your immune system as they enhance white cell development, which are key to protecting against invading micro-organisms. Mushrooms will also provide good anti-inflammatory benefits to the body and will also provide antioxidant support as well. For those that are concerned about heart health, mushrooms can help to decrease the level of bad cholesterol and triglycerides in the body while increasing the level of healthy cholesterol. Finally, they're also slightly higher in protein content, which is a terrific option for anyone implementing a vegetarian diet.

# Mustard Greens

Mustard greens are a very powerful cholesterol lowering food, as they help to bind bile acids in your digestive track. Mustard greens offer strong cancer protection and will also supply a good dose of vitamin K, vitamin A, vitamin C, and folate. Adding these to your diet can help reduce the harmful effects of stress on the body and help protect against bladder cancer, as noted by a study published in the Cancer Research Journal.

# Oak leaf lettuce

Oak leaf lettuce is an alternative form of lettuce that you can use in your salads to add more variety and enhance your nutrient consumption. Oak leaf lettuce is rich in beta-carotene, providing 247% of your total daily requirement. In addition to that, it's also high in zeaxanthin, which is a carotenoid that will help protect the eyes, and prevent age related macular degeneration. Finally, oak leaf lettuce is also rich in vitamin K and will reduce the negative effects associated with Alzheimer's disease.

# Olives

Olives are higher in total fat content, but its healthy fat so it will prevent heart disease, improve your cholesterol profile, and help prevent cancer, as noted by a study published in the European Journal of Cancer Prevention. In addition to that, olives can help promote stronger bones by increasing the total calcium absorption while decreasing the amount of bone mass loss over time. Olives also contain up to a quarter of your daily iron needs in just a one-cup serving, and this iron will help to ensure that you wont quickly fatigue in any physical activity that you perform.

# Onions

Onions add a very nice amount of flavor to any dish you're preparing and offer a good dose of polyphenol content. The regular consumption of onions can help enhance the bone and connective tissue development in the body and may be of particular benefit for women who are experiencing menopause, as it can help them to decrease their risk of hip fractures. Additionally, onions can help to reduce the level of inflammation in the body, which can then decrease your risk of heart disease and diabetes development.

# Oranges

Oranges are very well known for their vitamin C content, so they'll act as a potent antioxidant for anyone looking to improve their immune system and ward off viruses. Oranges will provide you with a decent amount of dietary fiber each day and will also supply vitamin B1, potassium, vitamin A, as well as a small dose of calcium to help support strong bones.

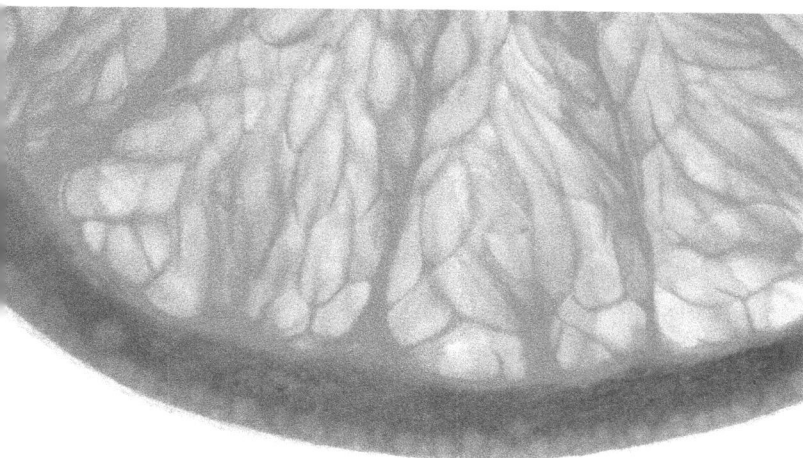

# Papaya

Another food that's very high in vitamin C content is papaya. Papaya is rich in dietary fiber, will provide 31% of your total vitamin A requirements with a one cup serving, and will also provide you with a small amount of calcium and folate as well. Papayas are great seasonal fruits to turn to any time you need a quick change in your diet plan.

# Paprika

Paprika is a great spice for enhancing the flavor of your foods and offering sound nutrition. It's incredibly low in sodium content coming in at just 2 mg per 6 gram serving, and will provide you with thiamin, magnesium, phosphorus, copper, vitamin C, A, E K, B6, and a small amount of iron and potassium as well. Paprika will even provide one gram of protein per 6 gram serving, along with 3 grams of dietary fiber and can reduce inflammatory conditions, as noted by a study published in the Annals of Rheumatic Diseases.

# Parsnip

If you are looking to increase your dietary fiber consumption, adding parsnip to your daily diet is one of the best ways to go about doing so. Parsnip contains 7 grams of fiber per one cup serving and won't provide any fat or cholesterol at all. It also offers 38% of your total vitamin C requirement and will provide 4% of your iron intake and 5% of your calcium requirements as well.

# Parsley

Parsley is often said to help enhance digestive system health and at 22 grams per cup, it's one food that you can add into your diet any time you please. Parsley is rich in dietary fiber coming in at 2 grams with one gram of sugar, and 2 grams of protein. Parsley will provide you with a good dose of vitamin E, thiamin, riboflavin, niacin, vitamin B6, as well as vitamin A, C, and vitamin K. Add this any time to your meals when you need a quick nutritional boost.

# Passion fruit

Passion fruit is a form of fruit that is slightly higher in calories compared to most coming in at 229 per one cup serving. It does still boast many health benefits however, so this does not mean you should avoid adding it to your diet. You simply need to be smart about your serving size. Passion fruit is a great source of dietary fiber at 25 grams per serving, will provide 5 grams of protein, is free from saturated and trans fats, and will supply over 100% of your vitamin C requirements. Additionally, it's also a great way to get potassium in to foster strong workout sessions.

# Pears

Pears are a nice treat when you need a change from apples, and are rich in both dietary fiber, as well as vitamin C. Pears can help provide very strong protection against free radical damage due to their high vitamin C as well as copper content. In addition to this, pears will also help support a healthy colon due to their fiber content. This fiber can also help to lower your overall cholesterol levels, reducing your risk of heart atherosclerosis and heart disease.

# Peppermint

One great way that you can help reduce your appetite level, making it easier to stick with a fat loss diet, is to enjoy peppermint on a regular basis. Adding a bit of peppermint into your main dishes, or even into some tea to have before dinner is a great way to nourish your body without any calories. Peppermint is a good source of phosphorus, zinc, as well as dietary fiber, vitamin A, and vitamin C.

# Pineapple

Pineapples are one of the sweeter fruits that you can consume, and boast a very high vitamin C content, providing 131% of your total needs with just a one cup serving. Pineapple is a strong source of manganese, fiber, vitamin B6, copper, as well as vitamin B1, and will also help to provide folate to the body as well. Pineapples support a healthy digestive system due to the bromelain that they contain, which can also help to reduce the degree of inflammation present in the body. Finally, pineapple can also help defend against macular degeneration as well.

# Plums

Plums are a nice lower calorie fruit choice at 30 calories per piece, which makes them an easy addition to any meal or snack in your day. They contain vitamin C, vitamin K, as well as vitamin A and will also supply a small dose of fiber as well. When you eat plums on a regular basis in the body, you'll increase the absorption of iron, which will reduce the risk of suffering from iron-deficiency anemia.

# Pomegranate

Pomegranates have rapidly caught on as one of the superfruits that you should be eating, as they offer so many health benefits. For one medium pomegranate, you'll take in 234 calories, 3 grams of fat, some of which are essential fatty acids, as well as 11 grams of dietary fiber. Pomegranates are especially high in antioxidants and will protect you against free radical stress, really enhancing the overall health benefits that they provide. They're also a great source of folate, vitamin C, and vitamin K.

# Prunes

Prunes are a great food to eat when you need a high amount of energy quickly, as they are very calorie dense at 110 calories per quarter cup serving. For those who are doing intense physical activity, prunes are a terrific option to turn to. Prunes are high in antioxidant content and also provide a good degree of beta-carotene, which will decrease inflammation in the body and help defend against free radical damage. Despite their high calorie and sugar content, prunes contain soluble fiber, so they'll actually be very beneficial for normalizing your blood glucose levels.

# Pumpkin

Pumpkin is a food that most people only think of eating at Halloween, but it can offer clear health benefits at any point during the year. At 30 calories per cup, it's definitely classified as a low calorie food. Furthermore, it contains just one milligram of sodium, so is ideal for those who want to promote maximum heart health. Finally, pumpkin is also a good source of thiamin, niacin, vitamin B6, folate, and magnesium. Try it outside of a pie for the best overall health benefits.

# Potatoes

Potatoes often get a bad rap for being higher up on the glycemic index, but if you serve them up with a lean source of protein and some healthy fats, they won't spike your blood glucose nearly as much as you may believe. Potatoes are high in potassium, so will support optimal energy levels especially during physical activity and are also rich in vitamin C, vitamin B6, and tryptophan. Potatoes can also help to lower blood pressure levels, reducing your risk of heart disease and stroke.

# Radish

Radishes are a lower calorie food, coming in at just 19 calories per one cup serving and will supply you with vitamin C, folate, potassium, vitamin B6, magnesium, as well as copper. What's more is that they'll offer 2 grams of dietary fiber, so they can calm your hunger quickly. Radishes taste great when added to a salad, so make sure that you don't overlook them.

# Radicchio

Radicchio is incredibly low in calories at just 9 per one cup serving and is a great way to bulk up your diet without risking any weight gain. Radicchio is high in vitamin B6, pantothenic acid, iron, magnesium, as well as phosphorus and zinc, and is also a terrific source of vitamin C and E. Mix it in with any other lettuce varieties that you enjoy and you'll have a great spin on your usual salad.

# Raisins

Another snack that's excellent to eat when you need a good dose of energy quickly is raisins. Raisins are high in calories coming in at 108 per quarter cup serving, but they will help support strong bones. Raisins contain boron, which is a trace mineral that helps convert estrogen and vitamin D into their most active forms, which is precisely what's needed to help maintain high bone density. In addition to that, raisins will also provide strong antioxidant protection, very similar to grapes.

# Raspberries

Raspberries are one of the best berries that you can consume on a regular basis, as they are very low in sugar content, high in dietary fiber, and low in calories as well. Raspberries do offer a more tart taste than most other berries, so mix them into other foods if you prefer. They contain vitamin C, manganese, fiber, as well as vitamin K. At 63 calories per cup, you can't go wrong adding them into your day.

# Red pepper

Red peppers are an excellent way to strengthen your immune system because they contain a very high amount of total vitamin C content. In addition to that, they're also going to offer strong anti-inflammatory benefits to the body and can help to reduce the level of inflammation you experience as well. One important thing to note about red peppers is that it appears that the cooking process does destroy some of the nutrients they contain, so consume them raw whenever possible.

# Romaine lettuce

A healthier option than using iceberg lettuce in your salad (due to its higher nutrient content) is romaine lettuce. This lettuce variety contains over 100% of your total vitamin A and vitamin K requirement and is also a great source of vitamin C, folate, as well as dietary fiber. Romaine lettuce can help to reduce the risk of plaque formation along the arteries, reducing the risk of heart attack or stroke.

# Rosemary

Rosemary is another great herb that can be used to flavor your foods when you don't want to add any excess calories or sodium, and is going to help promote your overall well-being. Rosemary is high in vitamin B6, magnesium, potassium, copper, and is also a great source of vitamin A, vitamin, C, folate, calcium, and iron. Sprinkle it on top of salads or fish for added flair.

# Sage

Speaking of spices, don't overlook sage. Sage will provide you with one gram of dietary fiber per tablespoon you use, which will reduce the impact the meal has on your blood glucose level. In addition to that, it's also a good source of vitamin B6, folate, calcium, iron, and vitamin E, and will strengthen your immune system as well as defend against free radical damage.

# Seaweed

Seaweed is one rare vegetable that many people never think of adding to their diet, and one that can offer some spectacular health benefits. Seaweed contains just 13 calories per ounce and doesn't contain any sugar. Seaweed is a good source of vitamin A, vitamin C, vitamin E, as well as phosphorus, and will also provide you with a small dose of iron and magnesium as well.

# Snow peas

Snow peas are a great vegetable to add to your salads, stir-fry's, or just to steam and serve separately on the side of your main dish. Snow peas are low in calories at just 41 per cup serving and are also high in protein for a vegetable, coming in at 3 grams per serving. In addition to that, you'll get three grams of fiber along with a good dose of riboflavin, vitamin B6, pantothenic acid, magnesium, phosphorus, potassium, and dietary fiber.

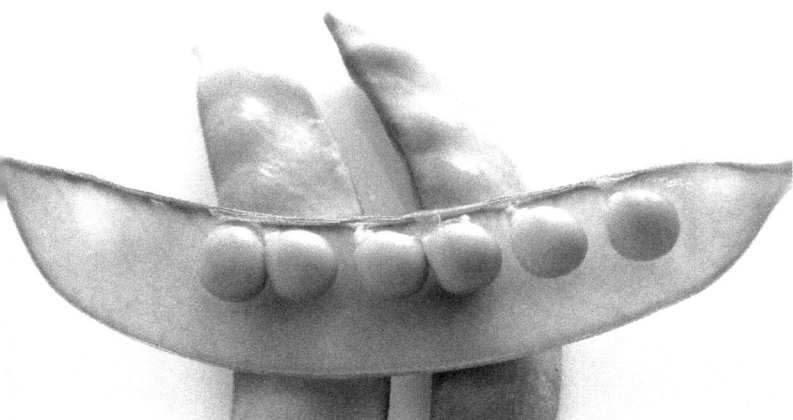

# Spaghetti squash

Spaghetti squash makes for a fantastic alternative for those who are looking to cut their carbohydrate intake but don't want to give up pasta. This vegetable closely mimics pasta and will work great mixed with any tomato based sauce with some veggies. Spaghetti squash is high in vitamin C, molybdenum, vitamin B6, as well as manganese, and is also going to provide you with a good dose of folate and fiber as well. Unlike pasta, which can increase your blood glucose levels, this veggie is more likely to keep them on an even keel.

# Spinach

Spinach is one of the most nutrient dense leaf varieties that you can possibly consume, and is going to pack in a high amount of excellent nutrition for your body. Spinach is well known for its iron content, and a great choice for anyone who is a vegetarian. In addition to this, it's also high in vitamin C, which will help foster a stronger immune system, and help decrease the effects of stress on the body. Spinach can help to reduce your risk of developing cancer, while also providing clear anti-inflammatory benefits to those who regularly include it in their diet.

# Strawberries

Strawberries contain a very potent dose of vitamin C, providing well over 100% of your daily needs and will also promote a strong cardiovascular system as well. In addition to that, strawberries can regulate your blood sugar levels due to their fiber content, so anyone who is looking to manage their blood glucose levels should consider adding them into their diet. Finally, strawberries can also enhance your cognitive function, so if you're preparing for a mentally taxing activity, consider eating some beforehand.

# Summer squash

Summer squash is a great way to get in some high fiber carbohydrates that will produce a slow and steady increase in energy levels. Lower in calories than pasta and potatoes, summer squash works great as an alternative for those following a fat loss diet. It contains a high amount of vitamin C, molybdenum, vitamin B6, potassium, vitamin B2, as well as folate and dietary fiber. This food is also great for offering strong prostate health support, so it's a particularly great choice for males and can help improve your rate of lipid metabolism, as noted by a study published in 2007.

# Swiss chard

Swiss chard is very high in phytonutrients and will help to eliminate toxins in the body while also keeping your blood sugar levels under control. Swiss chard is incredibly high in vitamin K, providing over 700% of your daily requirements in a one-cup serving, and is also a rich source of vitamin A, vitamin C, magnesium, manganese, and potassium. It will even supply 22% of your daily requirement for iron, so is a great way to ensure that you sustain high energy levels.

# Tomatoes

Tomatoes are well known for the lycopene content and are especially great for men looking to keep their prostate healthy, but they will also promote a healthier heart as well. Tomatoes are high in antioxidants, and due to the vitamin C and E combination they contain, are especially helpful for warding off atherosclerosis. In addition to that, tomatoes can also assist with the regulation of fats in the blood, therefore can help to keep your overall triglyceride levels healthier as well.

# Turnips

Turnips are a food that is low in calories at 34 per cup and will pack in a high amount of dietary fiber, containing 3 grams per serving. They are slightly higher in sugar content for a vegetable coming in at 5 grams per serving, but this will be offset by the dietary fiber. In addition to that, turnips are also cholesterol free and are a great source of vitamin B6, calcium, and manganese.

# Turnip greens

Turnip greens stand out for their high calcium content, as they contain up to four times as much calcium per serving as other greens do. This will help to promote stronger bones, and also help to keep your muscular contractions regulated. Turnip greens are also rich in vitamin K, vitamin A, vitamin C, as well as folate, manganese, and fiber. Finally, this food can go a long way towards detoxing your body and providing optimal health support.

# Watermelon

Watermelon is a great sweet treat on a hot summer's day. Watermelon will not contribute many calories to your diet, and due to its high water content, will help keep you hydrated. Watermelon is a good source of vitamin C, vitamin A, potassium, as well as magnesium, and will provide antioxidants that help to strengthen the heart, and blood vessel walls.

# Wasabi

If you want a fast way to add a whole lot of spice to your meals, try wasabi. Used traditionally in oriental cooking, it's low in calories and high in dietary fiber. This food is completely cholesterol free so is great for those trying to promote heart health. In addition to that, it's also a good source of vitamin B6 and calcium. Be sure to look for the real wasabi root, as most wasabi is nothing more than horseradish, food coloring, and flavouring.

# Watercress

Watercress is perhaps one of the lowest calorie vegetables coming in at just four per cup and will actually provide a good source of protein in your diet. While you won't get much protein from eating this food being that it is so low in calories, most of the calories it contains will come from the protein content. In addition to that, it's also a great source of vitamin A, vitamin C, and vitamin E.

# Winter squash

Winter squash can be utilized in your diet a number of ways, including eating the squash itself, or eating the seeds for some healthy fats. These seeds will provide you with important linoleic acids, which are required for optimal brain and heart health. The carbohydrates in winter squash come mostly from pectin, which is a certain type of carbohydrate that will slow down digestion and induce high feelings of satiety. In addition to that, it also can help prevent diabetes.

# Yams

Yams are a great alternative to potatoes and have a nice sweet taste to them while being a very good source of vitamin C. They're also rich in potassium, which means they are a good option to have before your workout session. Furthermore, at 157 calories per cup, they're slightly lower in calories compared to pasta or brown rice.

So there you have it. 101 of the top plant based foods to add to your diet. As you can see, your options are plentiful. Many people feel that if they cut out meat and processed foods, they'll have limited food selection. This couldn't be farther from the truth! There is a cornucopia of wonderful foods out there just waiting for you.

Regardless of what your taste preferences are, you'll easily be able to come up with a varied diet plan that delivers sound nutrition, and taste, time and time again.

So don't wait any longer to take this leap forward to improve your health. Adopt a plant-based diet today and you'll start feeling better because of it tomorrow.

# Where to Find the 101 Best Whole Foods In Your Grocery Store

Below you will find the foods listed in a section where you might find them in a grocery store. Some items may be found in more than one place in your store so that is why you will find them listed in more than one section below. Whenever possible … eat FRESH or Frozen … not canned or preserved. Enjoy!

## PRODUCE DEPARTMENT

Apples

Apricots

Asparagus

Arugula

Artichoke

Avocados

Banana

Bamboo shoots

Basil

Beets

Bell peppers

Blackberries

Blackcurrant

Bean sprouts

Beet root

Bok Choy

Boysenberries

Blueberries

Broccoli

Broccolini

Brussels sprouts

Butter Leaf lettuce

Cabbage

Cantaloupe

Carrots

Cauliflower

Celery

Cherry

Chicory

Chili pepper

Chinese broccoli

Chinese cabbage

Chives

Collard greens

Corn

Crab-apple

Cranberry

Cucumber

Current

Dill

Eggplant

Fennel

FigsKiwi

Grapefruit

Grapes

Gooseberry

Green beans

Green peas

Green pepper

Honeydew

Iceberg lettuce

Kale

Leeks

Lemon

Limes

Lychee

Mandarins

Mushrooms

Mustard Greens

Oak leaf lettuce

Olives

Onions

Oranges

Papaya

Paprika

Parsnip

Parsley

Passion fruit

Pears

Peppermint

Pineapple

Plums

Pomegranate

Prunes

Pumpkin

Potatoes

Radish

Radicchio

Raisins

Raspberries

Red pepper

Romaine lettuce

Rosemary

Sage

Seaweed

Snow peas

Spaghetti squash

Spinach

Strawberries

Summer squash

Swiss chard

Tomatoes

Turnips

Turnip greens

Watermelon

Wasabi

Watercress

Winter squash

Yams

## HEALTH FOOD SECTION

Acai Berries

## FROZEN FOOD

Asparagus

Artichoke

Blackberries

Blueberries

Broccoli

Brussels sprouts

Carrots

Cauliflower

Corn

Green beans

Green peas

Potatoes

Raspberries

Spinach

Strawberries

# Plant-Based Eating Can Reap Rewards

*News from The National Institute of Health*

Vegetarians miss out on lots of foods. No grilled burgers or franks at picnics. No holiday turkey or fries cooked in animal fat. Strict vegetarians may even forego honey made by bees. But vegetarians also tend to miss out on major health problems that plague many Americans. They generally live longer than the rest of us, and they're more likely to bypass heart-related and other ailments.

The fact is, eating a more plant-based diet can boost your health, whether you're a vegetarian or not.

What is it about the vegetarian lifestyle that can protect your health? And are there risks to being vegetarian? NIH-funded researchers are looking for answers. They're exploring the many ways that diet and other factors affect our health.

Vegetarian meals focus on fruits and vegetables, dried beans, whole grains, seeds and nuts. By some estimates, about 2% of the U.S. adult population follows this type of diet.

People have many reasons for becoming vegetarians. Some want to eat more healthy foods. Others have religious or economic reasons or are concerned about animal welfare. "Vegetarian diets are also more sustainable and environmentally sound than diets that rely heavily on meat, poultry and fish," says NIH nutritionist Dr. Susan Krebs-Smith, who monitors trends in cancer risk factors.

Most people think of vegetarian diets as simply eating plant foods and not eating meat, poultry and fish. "But in fact, there are many different types of vegetarian diets," Krebs-Smith explains. "Some are more restrictive than others."

Strict vegetarians, or vegans, eat plant foods and reject all animal products—meat, poultry, fish, eggs, dairy and sometimes honey. Those who also eat dairy products are called lacto vegetarians. Vegetarians who eat both dairy and eggs are called lacto-ovo vegetarians.

Some vegetarians eat fish but not meat or poultry. They're called pescatarians (pesce is Italian for fish).

"Then there are the so-called flexitarians, or semi-vegetarians. These are people who eat a mostly vegetarian diet, but they occasionally eat meat," says Jody Engel, a nutritionist and registered dietitian at NIH. "They might say 'I'm a vegetarian, but I need to eat my burgers every Sunday.' People tend to follow their own rules, which is one reason why it's hard for researchers to study vegetarians. There's so much variance."

Despite the different definitions, "there's tremendous agreement among nutrition experts and health organizations that a more plant-based diet is beneficial, whether you're a true vegetarian or not," says Krebs-Smith. "Most Americans don't eat enough fruit, vegetables, legumes or whole grains. There's a huge consensus that eating more of these foods would be a good idea for everyone."

Vegetarian diets tend to have fewer calories, lower

levels of saturated fat and cholesterol, and more fiber, potassium and vitamin C than other eating patterns. Vegetarians tend to weigh less than meat-eaters, and to have lower cancer rates. "Evidence also suggests that a vegetarian diet is associated with a lower risk of death from certain heart diseases, and that those who follow a vegetarian diet tend to have lower LDL ["bad"] cholesterol levels," says Engel.

In some cases, though, it's unclear if certain health benefits come from plant-based eating or from the healthy lifestyle of most vegetarians. "Vegetarians are generally more physically active and have healthier habits than non-vegetarians. They also typically have a higher socioeconomic status, at least in the United States," says Krebs-Smith.

To tease out the effects of diet, scientists have to conduct large, carefully controlled studies that account for other factors. One of the world's largest studies of plant-based diets is now underway at Loma Linda University in California. Cardiologist Dr. Gary Fraser is leading an NIH-funded team of scientists to analyze data on 96,000 Seventh-day Adventists in all 50 states and in Canada. Members of this religious group have unique dietary habits and a generally healthy lifestyle.

Adventists are encouraged to follow a vegetarian diet, but about half the population sometimes eats meat. These variable eating patterns allow scientists to compare a wide range of dietary habits and look for links between diet and disease.

To date, the researchers have found that the closer

people are to being vegetarian, the lower their risk of diabetes, high blood pressure and metabolic syndrome (a condition that raises your risk for heart disease and stroke). "The trend is almost like a stepladder, with the lowest risks for the strict vegetarians, then moving up for the lacto vegetarians and then the pescatarians and then the non-vegetarians," Fraser explains. Earlier studies found that vegetarian Adventists also tend to live longer than both meat-eating Adventists and non-Adventists. The vegetarians also have less coronary heart disease and lower rates of some cancers.

Because vegetarians by definition don't eat meat, some people jump to the conclusion that simply cutting meat from your diet will lead to health benefits. "But it's actually more complicated than that," says Fraser. "Differences in life expectancy and other health matters might be related to the extra fruits, vegetables, nuts and legumes—including soy—that vegetarians tend to eat. You can't necessarily conclude it's based on the absence of meat," he says.

Experts generally agree that vegetarians who eat a wide variety of foods can readily meet all their body's needs for nutrients. "At any stage of life, you should be able to eat a healthy diet by consuming vegetarian foods. But it does take a little planning," says Rachel Fisher, a registered dietitian involved in nutrition research at NIH.

Vegetarians need to be sure they take in enough iron, calcium, zinc and vitamin B12. Studies show that most vegetarians do get enough, in part because so many cereals, breads and other foods are fortified with these nutrients. "Vegans in particular need to be certain to get enough vitamin B12 and omega-3 fatty acids," says Fisher. Omega-3, found in fish, flax seed, walnuts and canola oil, is important for heart health and vision.

Some vegetarians take dietary supplements to make sure they're getting everything they need. It's a good idea to talk to a registered dietitian or other health professional if you're a vegetarian or thinking of becoming one.

Whether you're a vegetarian or not, Fisher says, you can benefit from the high fiber, low fat and rich nutrients of a vegetarian diet. "Vegetarian foods can be so delicious, and they're so good for you," she says.

Try using a variety of spices and herbs to make things interesting. And make sure not to overcook your vegetables, or they might lose some of their valuable nutrients.

# Tips For Eating Healthy When Eating Out

- As a beverage choice, ask for water or order fat-free or low-fat milk, unsweetened tea, or other drinks without added sugars.

- Ask for whole-wheat bread for sandwiches.

- In a restaurant, start your meal with a salad packed with veggies, to help control hunger and feel satisfied sooner.

- Ask for salad dressing to be served on the side. Then use only as much as you want.

- Choose main dishes that include vegetables, such as stir fries, kebobs, or pasta with a tomato sauce.

- Order steamed, grilled, or broiled dishes instead of those that are fried or sautéed.

- Choose a small" or "medium" portion. This includes main dishes, side dishes, and beverages.

- Order an item from the menu instead heading for the "all-you-can-eat" buffet.

- If main portions at a restaurant are larger than you want, try one of these strategies to keep from overeating:

  * Order an appetizer-sized portion or a side dish instead of an entrée.

  * Share a main dish with a friend.

* If you can chill the extra food right away, take leftovers home in a "doggy bag."

* When your food is delivered, set aside or pack half of it to go immediately.

* Resign from the "clean your plate club" - when you've eaten enough, leave the rest.

- To keep your meal moderate in calories, fat, and sugars:

   * Ask for salad dressing to be served "on the side" so you can add only as much as you want.

   * Order foods that do not have creamy sauces or gravies

   * Add little or no butter to your food.

   * Choose fruits for dessert most often.

On long commutes or shopping trips, pack some fresh fruit, cut-up vegetables, low-fat string cheese sticks, or a handful of unsalted nuts to help you avoid stopping for sweet or fatty snacks.

---

*Courtesy U.S. Department of Agriculture*

# References

Agarwal, Amit, et al. (2006). Antioxidant Capacity and Other Bioactivities of the Freeze-Dried Amazonian Palm Berry. Journal of Agricultural and Food Chemistry. 54(22), pp. 8604-8610.

Alberto Ascherio et al. (1996). Prospective Study of Nutritional Factors, Blood Pressure, and Hypertension Among US Women. Hypertension. 27:1065-1072.

Bhattacharya A, Tang L, Li Y, et al. Inhibition of bladder cancer development by allyl isothiocyanate. Carcinogenesis. 2010 Feb;31(2):281-6. 2010.

Choi H, Eo H, Park K et al. A water-soluble extract from Cucurbita moschata shows anti-obesity effects by controlling lipid metabolism in a high fat diet-induced obesity mouse model. Biochem Biophys Res Commun. 2007 Aug

Goldbohm, R. A. (1996). Epidemiological studies on brassica vegetables and cancer risk. Cancer Epidemiology, Biomarkers & Prevention. 5, 733.

Hale-Shukitt, B. et al. (2008). Berry Fruit Supplementation and the Aging Brain. 56(3), pp. 636-641.

Hirano, T. et al. (1999). Ameliogoratory effect of dietary ingestion with red bell pepper on learning impairment in senescence-accelerated mice (SAMP8).

Jorge PA, Neyra LC, Osaki RM, et al. Effect of eggplant on plasma lipid levels, lipidic peroxidation and reversion of endothelial dysfunction in experimental hypercholesterolemia. Arq Bras Cardiol. 1998 Feb;70(2):87-91 1998.

Konoshima, T. et al. (1996). Chemoprevention of lung and skin cancer by Beta Vulgaris root extract. Cancer Letters. Vol. 100, Issue 1-2: pp. 211-214.

Kountouri AM, Kaliora AC, Koumbi L et al. In-vitro gastric cancer prevention by a polyphenol-rich extract from olives through induction of apoptosis. Eur J Cancer Prev. 2009 Feb;18(1):33-9. 2009..

Kwon YI, Apostolidis E, Kim YC et al. Health benefits of traditional corn, beans, and pumpkin: in vitro studies for hyperglycemia and hypertension management. J Med Food. 2007 Jun;10(2):266-75. 2007.

Pattison DJ, Silman AJ, Goodson NJ, Lunt M, Bunn D, Luben R, Welch A, Bingham S, Khaw KT, Day N, Symmons DP. Vitamin C and the risk of developing inflammatory polyarthritis: prospective nested case-control study. Ann Rheum Dis. 2004 Jul;63(7):843-7. 2004. PMID:15194581.

Tang L, Zirpoli GR, Guru K et al. Consumption of Raw Cruciferous Vegetables is Inversely Associated with Bladder Cancer Risk. Cancer Res. 2007 Apr 15;67(8):3569-73. 2007.

Turner, Vanamala J, Leonardi T, Patil B, Murphy M, Wang N, Pike L, et al. Grapefruit and its isolated bioactive compounds act as colon cancer chemoprotectants in rats. The 228th ACS National Meeting, Philadelphia, PA, August 24, 2004. 2004.

Xiao HB, Jun-Fang, Lu XY et al. Protective effects of kaempferol against endothelial damage by an improvement in nitric oxide production and a decrease in asymmetric dimethylarginine level. European Journal of PharmacologyVolume 616, Issues 1-3, 15 August 2009, Pages 213-222. 2009.